WAKE-UP CALLS

OTHER BOOKS BY THE SAME AUTHORS

Love Is Letting Go of Fear
Teach Only Love
Goodbye to Guilt
Out of the Darkness Into the Light
Love Is the Answer: Creating Positive Relationships
To Give Is to Receive: An 18-Day Mini-Course in Healing Relationships
One Person Can Make a Difference
Change Your Mind: Change Your Life

and for children
Me First and the Gimme Gimmes

AUDIO CASSETTES

Love Is Letting Go of Fear
Teach Only Love
Goodbye to Guilt
Creating Positive Relationships
To Give Is to Receive
Forgiveness Is the Key to Happiness
Introduction to A Course in Miracles
One Person Can Make a Difference
The Quiet Mind
Achieving Inner Peace
Visions of the Future I
Finding the Miracle of Love in Your Life:
Based on A Course in Miracles

VIDEO CASSETTES

Achieving Inner and Outer Success
Healing Relationships
Visions of the Future I

If you wish information on Jerry Jampolsky and Diane Cirincione's lec-
ture and workshop schedule, or if you wish to purchase books, audio
or video cassette tapes, please send a self-addressed envelope to P.O. Box
1012, Tiburon, CA 94920 or call 1-800-359-2246.

WAKE-UP
CALLS

GERALD G. JAMPOLSKY, M.D.
DIANE V. CIRINCIONE

Hay House, Inc.
Carson, CA

WAKE-UP CALLS
by Gerald G. Jampolsky, M.D. and Diane V. Cirincione

Library of Congress Cataloging-in-Publication Data

Jampolsky, Gerald G., 1925–
    Wake-up calls / Gerald G. Jampolsky, Diane V. Cirincione.
        p.   cm.
    ISBN 1–56170–055–X (hard) : $15.00
    1. Course in miracles. 2. Peace of mind—Religious aspects.
    3. Affirmations. I. Cirincione, Diane V. II. Title.
    BP605.C68J36   1992
    299'.93—dc20   92–23344
                                                         CIP

ISBN: 1–56170–055–X
Library of Congress Catalog Card No. 92–23344

Internal Design by Freedmen's Organization
Typesetting by Freedmen's Typesetting Organization, Los Angeles, CA 90004

92 93 94 95 96 97   10 9 8 7 6 5 4 3 2 1
First Printing, October 1992

Published and Distributed in the United States by:

Hay House, Inc.
P.O. Box 6204
Carson, CA 90749-6204
USA

Printed in the United States of America

DEDICATION

This book is dedicated to the many individuals who have volunteered their services by devoting part of their lives to helping others in the eighty-five independent Centers for Attitudinal Healing located around the world.

They have given freely and openly to others and have discovered giving and receiving are one and the same. Through their volunteer service they are being awakened to Love.

They serve as witnesses to the power of Love and demonstrate that giving can be a way of living. May these awakening Souls be "Guiding Lights" to us all.

ACKNOWLEDGMENTS

We wish to acknowledge with heartfelt thanks Jim Leary and Reid Tracy of Hay House Publishing who gave us their encouragement, enthusiasm, and support during the writing of this book, and to Betty Karr, our dear friend, who typed this manuscript. We wish to also acknowledge and give thanks to our dear friends, Hal and Dorothy Thau, who offered many helpful suggestions.

We also wish to share our continued love and gratitude to Judith Skutch Whitson and Bob Skutch, publishers of *A Course in Miracles*, for their permission to quote from this material, which continues to be an inspiration in our lives and our writings. When there is a direct quote from *A Course in Miracles*, you will find it noted by an *. There are a few anonymous quotes that will be noted by **.

INTRODUCTION

Wherever we travel in the world we are observing an awakening in people to a message from within. A "wake-up" call seems to beckon them to arise as if from a deep sleep of aimless dreams where they felt lost and have forgotten that who and what they are is Love.

The call from within gently offers that there must be another way of looking at the world; another way of living; another way of believing and thinking; and, there must be a way of having a meaningful life where we all can live with an abundance of Love and an absence of fear. The "wake up" call is a call to live in harmony and cooperation, to live a life of simplicity and balance rather than one of complexity and chaos.

In spite of a world often filled with confusion and despair, there are many who are finding new and creative ways of committing their lives to giving and helping others; a life of activating spiritual principles in practical ways in every day living.

They are learning to let go of their fears about the

past and their worries about the future and to live in the eternal moment of now. They treasure the moments of stillness rather than the moments of busyness. They are peaceful because their minds are devoid of conflictual thoughts. They bring light to a darkened world. Their lives are statements of their beliefs as they are motivated with an integrity, consistency, and honesty in what they think, say, and do. They, indeed, walk their talk.

As we look back at the past, has there been anyone amongst us who has not been caught up in the busyness of the world only to end up hurried, harried, confused, tired, weary, frustrated, angry, lonely, afraid and fearful? Many of us at one time or another, have perceived the world as being unfair, where we have often felt like innocent victims of someone else's crimes.

The fuel for the world, in general, has been blame and self-condemnation under a guise of a perceived need to proliferate, "attack" and "defense". We have had a belief system where catastrophes, wars and starvation would continue to happen. It has often encompassed the belief that stated death was the end of the line; that we were always in danger of rejection, being abandoned and isolated, and where many of us ended up numb and unable to feel our own emotional pulse.

For many of us it has been a world of worry and conflict where fear, not love, played a dominant role; where we became afraid of Love and intimacy; and where frequent concerns about getting hurt were just around the next corner of time.

It has been a world in which it was difficult to find words to explain how we felt inside. In spite of our successes there was a feeling of emptiness inside, a feeling of spiritual deprivation that questioned that there must be more to life than this. There has been a growing, inner hunger and craving for a sense of spiritual fulfillment that all the things in our outer world never seemed to satisfy.

Hopefully, this small book will be able to contribute some practical, healthy food that will satisfy the "spiritual hunger" that so many of us are feeling today and serve to remove the blocks to the awareness of Love's presence. May it help awaken us from our illusions of separation and our dreams of anger, hate, blame, self-condemnation and despair.

May these "wake-up" calls remind us that we are all interconnected, joined as one through the Source that created us, and that we can become free once again when we remember that we are not here to judge, but to Love. It is a Love that is unconditional, has no exceptions, no expectations nor assumptions; it makes no judgments and simply and forever continues to unfold upon itself.

The time has come for each of us to awaken and remember that no matter what the question, Love is the answer. It is a "wake-up" call to remember God and to remember that in the real world we are Love; the miracle of Love is within us; Love is everything, and there is nothing else but Love.

Jerry Jampolsky   Diane Cirincione

WAKE-UP CALLS

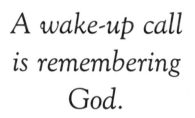

*A wake-up call
is remembering
God.*

Today I choose to remember the loving Source that created me.

Remembering God, or whatever you choose to call the Loving force that created us, is what "waking up" is all about. It is remembering that Love is what created us and, therefore, Love is what we are. It is remembering that we are spiritual beings, who were created as the essence of Love.

Little Child,
you think you are chained
to your shadow.
It is but a dream.
Awaken
and you will see
that you are free.

**I will awaken today and
let go of the chains
to the shadows of my past.**

Our egos would have us walk with chewing gum on the soles of our shoes, always keeping the past stuck to our feet. The hurtful past is the ego's ball and chain that keeps us imprisoned. When we awaken, the shadow of our past disappears and with it, the ball and chain.

To be awake

is

to know

that we are never separate.

Today I am determined to see the interconnectedness of all of life.

It is thoughts of Love that bind us and thoughts of fear that cause us to feel separation. Let us be willing to take a leap in faith and trust to believe that which created us is only a Loving Force. Let us accept the presence of this Love for ourselves, and our gratitude can be demonstrated by giving that Love to all others.

To be fully awake, let us do our best to let go of all judgments and fears. Let us feel no separation between our Source, ourselves, others, and all that is living as we remind ourselves that being fully awake is being fully alive with Love.

To awaken
is
to choose
"nowsight"
rather than
hindsight or foresight.

Today I will choose the vision of "nowsight."

Many of us suffer because we spend enormous energy thinking about all the things we think we could or should have done. We often become so engrossed in our fears and fantasies about what the future may or may not hold, we end up totally missing the present.

Love is ultimately only experienced in the present for this moment is the only time there is.

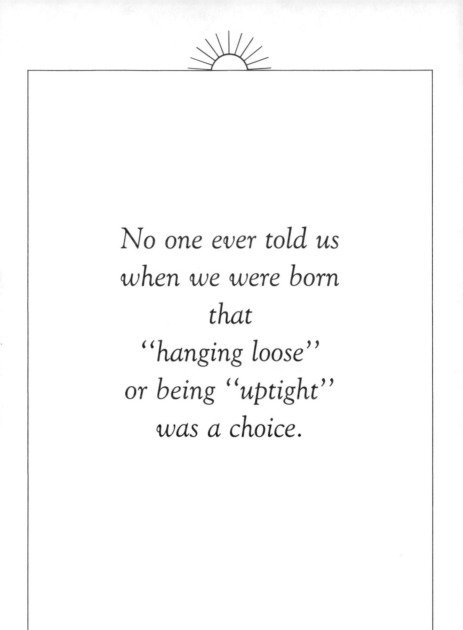

*No one ever told us
when we were born
that
"hanging loose"
or being "uptight"
was a choice.*

No matter what happens today, I am going to be willing to "hang loose."

Many of us believe that we are born with an "uptight" gene, destined to develop conditioned reflex behaviors where we become "uptight" around each and every stressful event that we face.

Let us remember that at any point in our lives we can choose to "hang loose" rather than become "uptight."

*If our hearts were open
to love,
we would
have less need
for open
heart surgery.*

**I will remind myself today
that I want to take responsibility
for my health;
and I will look at health as
inner peace and healing as the
letting go of fear.**

We tend to close our hearts off from others as well as ourselves when we believe we have been rejected. What frequently follows is that we become fearful of Love and end up holding on to anger and resentment in the futile belief that our anger will protect us. Instead, it finds a place to dwell in our bodies causing us sickness and ill health. As we open our hearts to healing, we begin to let go of fear.

*Waking up means losing
all desire to hurt
another person or ourselves.*

I will attempt to remember today that I can be happy when I have loving thoughts and actions towards others and myself.

We live in a world that says under certain circumstances it is alright and healthy to hurt others. It is a world that encourages us to be guilty, to punish ourselves and to hold on to unforgiving thoughts. It is a world that believes each of us should decide who is guilty and who is innocent.

Let us choose to change our belief systems and see no value in having hurtful attack thoughts or actions towards others or ourselves.

We have things backwards
because
"rest in peace" should
be for the
living and not the dead.

Today I choose to rest in peace.

Having peace, being at peace and resting in peace can be experienced in this present moment. It has nothing to do with the state of our body and has everything to do with our present state of mind.

Every moment has a stillness in which we can rest peacefully within, regardless of what is happening in the world outside. In each moment we can choose to rest peacefully within.

*There are only two emotions:
Love and fear.* *

Today I will choose to experience Love rather than fear and in so doing, I will be able to increase the levels of depth, intimacy, clarity and tenderness in all my relationships.

It is possible to live in this world as if there were only two emotions, Love and fear. We can learn to retrain our minds to believe that people are either loving or that they are fearful, giving us a call of help for Love. Anger, rage and violence are all aspects of fear.

Rather than perceiving another person as "attacking" us, we can choose to see that person as fearful and giving us a call for help. Our hearts will then be able to be compassionate towards that person, rather than "attacking" back. Once we decide not to attack back, we can go inside and ask what it is we need to think, say and do.

*Can it be that life depends
entirely on how
we choose to perceive it?*

Today I will remember that everything I perceive and experience will depend on what thoughts I choose to hold in my mind.

When we listen to the voice of the ego, we see things through the filter of fear. We see a fearful world and are prone to feel anxious, frightened and victimized. We can choose to see no value in holding onto the fearful, hurtful memories of the past. When we have only loving thoughts in our mind, we perceive only a loving world.

*A course that will lead your
ship safely home
has
the direction of
peace of mind
as
its only goal.*

Today my only goal will be peace of mind.

The way to a peaceful day is to not have conflicting, multiple goals for ourselves. We can keep things very simple today by having the singular goal of peace of mind and peace of God where the means and the end are the same.

*Fear is never dear
and always comes
from life's rear.*

I will remind myself that I can't experience Love and fear at the same time, and that this day is for letting go of the fearful past.

The ego mind stores excess baggage filled with old movies of the hurtful past. As we carry these old memories around, the present gets superimposed by all the old images from the past. We keep storing these old films because there is a part of our mind that sees value in fear; is attracted to fear; and would make us feel that fear benefits us in some way. Let us remember that fear is never in the present, but always related to something in the past, often projected onto the present and the future. When we stop seeing value in fear, we can then let go of our old baggage and experience the totality of Love once again.

*Awakening occurs
when
we recognize
that
there is never
anyone
to blame.*

Today I choose not to blame others or myself.

Have you ever thought about how much time is consumed each day with blaming others? The world we live in seems to have a popular belief that states, "If something goes wrong, find someone else to blame."

It is helpful to remember that every time we attack another person, we are really attacking ourselves.

When we make our intellect our God, we lose the experience of God.

Today I choose to see the world through my heart and not my intellect.

It is very easy to fall into the trap of seeing the world only through our intellect. We do this when at a deep level we are afraid. This results in our spending an enormous amount of time each day interpreting, analyzing, and judging each others' behavior, frequently leaving us with a lot of fear and an absence of Love.

When we realize that our intellect does not understand the experience of Love, we can choose to use our hearts as our filter in seeing the world.

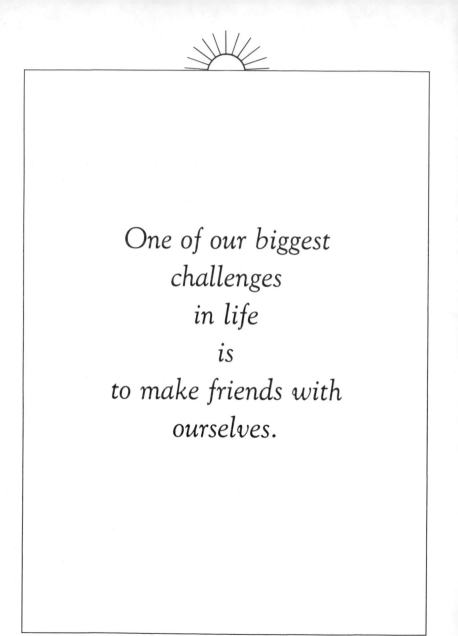

One of our biggest
challenges
in life
is
to make friends with
ourselves.

Today I will tear down all the barriers I have put up and make friends with myself.

The Pogo comic strip once said, "I went out to find the enemy and discovered it is me." But in truth there is no enemy. Our egos have built walls to hide the light that is always shining within. Let us embrace and shake hands with ourselves today as we welcome ourselves home in a truce of Love.

*Changing the thoughts
in our minds
can change our lives.*

**Today I will do my best to
remember that the solution
to any conflict
begins with changing the
thoughts in my mind.**

If for any reason today we feel attacked, rejected, or victimized, we can remember that
it is only our own thoughts that ultimately hurt
us. We can elect to change those thoughts at
any given moment and choose to see things
differently.

*One of the most difficult
challenges that human
beings have is to look into
the mirror and say,
"I love you with all my heart
just as you are."*

I will do my best to look in a mirror at least three times today and tell myself, "I love you with all my heart just as you are."

Many of us do not Love ourselves unconditionally. We do not accept ourselves and think we would be more lovable if our noses were smaller, our eyes were prettier, or that our ears were shaped differently. More importantly, we think we would be more lovable if we had behaved differently in the past.

We are lovable and deserving of Love today.

To awaken
and experience freedom
is
to let go of the
attachments we have
to all of our
possessions.

Today let me remember that it is only Love that can bring me peace and happiness.

We live in a world whose belief system equates possessions with happiness. Having possessions is fine as long as we don't rely on them to make us happy. Neither can we blame a lack of possessions for our unhappiness. It is never "things" that make us unhappy, but our attachments to them. We can be rich in material goods and poor in spirit and we can be poor in material goods and rich in spirit. As Mother Teresa has said, it is not how much we have or do in life that counts, but how much Love we have or do it with.

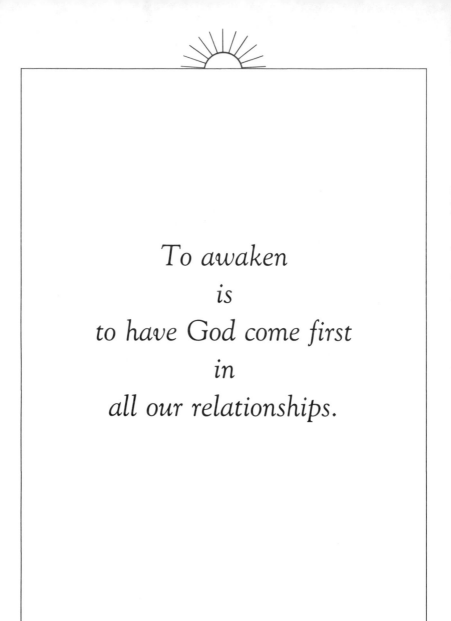

*To awaken
is
to have God come first
in
all our relationships.*

Today I am willing to let God come first in all my relationships.

Many of our relationships are built on having our own needs come first. They are built on scarcity where the illusion of Love is a bargain or a trade and they tend to end up as Love/hate relationships.

A Holy Relationship, on the other hand, is where two people come together as wholes, believing in the abundance of Love. They join their wills as one to be directed individually by their Inner Voice.

Attitudinal healing is based
on the premise
that it is not people or
situations in the past that
cause us to be upset.
It is ultimately our thoughts
and attitudes
about those people and
situations
in the present that cause us
distress.

I will remind myself that it is only my own thoughts that hurt me.

The things that hurt us in the past are not really hurting us now. What may be hurting us now are our thoughts about those things. Today, we can recognize that it has been our thoughts that have kept the hurtful past alive.

What causes us to lose our peace is not other people, but our own thoughts, judgments and attitudes about them. When we take responsibility for our own thoughts, the world we see begins to change.

*The thoughts we think create
the reality of what we see
and experience.
Taking responsibility for all of
our own thoughts will ultimately
change the world.*

I am responsible for everything I see. I choose the feelings I experience.*

Being responsible for what we see and experience does not imply blame which results in guilt. Instead, it empowers us to know that we are participating in creating our reality instead of being victims of the world around us.

The law of guilt is to punish yourself or someone else. The first step in letting go of guilt is to no longer see any value in holding onto it.

Today I plan to be loving by not putting guilt trips on others or myself.

Do you want to lighten your load in life? Do you want to rid yourself of backaches, headaches, and pains in your neck? Do you want to feel light-hearted and feel your sense of humor blossoming? Do you want to see anger, resentment and irritability vanish into the air? Do you want to see weariness and heaviness disappear? Do you want to feel more energy and a zest for living? The answer is that it is possible to have all this by discovering what it is you feel guilty about; why you have been choosing to hold onto it; and, finally letting go of the guilt.

Loving and pleasing
are not
the same thing.

Today I will not try to get people to like me by pleasing them.

Rather than trying to win a popularity contest, it is more loving to ourselves and others when we are honest in all of our communications. In trying to please other people we become unreal by shading our true feelings, which often emerge later in hostile form. It is our honesty that allows our Love to flow freely.

*Perception is a mirror
and not a fact.**

Today I will remember
that what I see in the world
is but a reflection
of the thoughts in my own mind.

What a different world we would see if each of us could recognize that it is our thoughts that create our reality. When we have angry thoughts, we see an angry world. When we have loving thoughts, we see a loving world. It is our belief system that determines what we see. What we see is based on what we believe and what we expect. As we take responsibility for what we perceive, the world we see will immediately reflect the change.

We need to recognize that our thoughts are as important as our actions and that a single thought has the power to transform the world.

Today I will constantly remind myself about the power of my own mind, and I will strive to have positive, caring and loving thoughts.

There are no big or small loving thoughts. All loving thoughts are the same, all powerful and capable of touching everything there is. As we recognize the power of our own thoughts, we will be much more responsible for the kind of thoughts we make in our minds. We can remind ourselves that our thoughts are powerful and that we and our thoughts do make a difference.

*If you don't want to be
one of your doctor's
many patients,
make it a priority in your life
to have infinite patience.*

I will see every person I meet as my teacher of infinite patience.

To be impatient is to be hooked on the future. It is to be in so much of a hurry that we give up the present. When we trust and have faith that God's Love is always within us, we can have infinite patience and know that where we are in the present is exactly where we need to be.

*Tenderness and
gentleness
walk hand in hand,
for where there
is no fear
there is only Love.*

Today I will teach tenderness and gentleness by demonstrating them in my life.

It has been said that only the very strong can ever dare to be gentle. When we choose not to see ourselves as attacked, we will not experience fear. Love is what we are and tenderness and gentleness are the very core of that Love.

Justified anger
never
brings us peace of mind.

**I will remember that anger
is part of our human condition
and is nothing to feel
guilty about.
When I feel anger, I will do
my best to honor it, to express it
in healthy ways, and then to see
no value in holding onto it.**

Anger is part of our human process and is neither bad nor good. It is what we do with the anger that gets us into trouble. Denying, repressing or dumping our anger onto others or ourselves only causes more conflict. We need to learn how to recognize when we are angry, and how to honor, explore, and find healthy ways of expressing it; and then to detach ourselves from the anger by no longer seeing any value in it. If we want to experience peace, it is helpful to remind ourselves that we cannot be attached to our anger and have peace of mind at the same time.

*Perhaps one of the most
important questions
we can ask ourselves before
talking is,
"Are my words going to bring
about joining or separation?"*

Let me remember
that the purpose
of all my relationships
is for joining.

M àny times our statements and questions to others are communications that attack and separate. Let us begin all of our conversations with the intention of experiencing joining with others.

*Celestial amnesia is
letting go of the past and
remembering only the Love
we have given and received.*

The past is gone and I can decide that it will no longer hurt me.

Have you ever tried celestial amnesia? It is guaranteed to ease you. It is letting go of all the hurtful past, and remembering only that Love lasts. Our dear friend, Bill Thetford, defined it as the kind of selective forgetting that allows us to let go of everything in the past except the Love that we have given and received. Celestial amnesia allows us to not let the hurtful past be superimposed on the present. This moment, then, becomes a reality of Love.

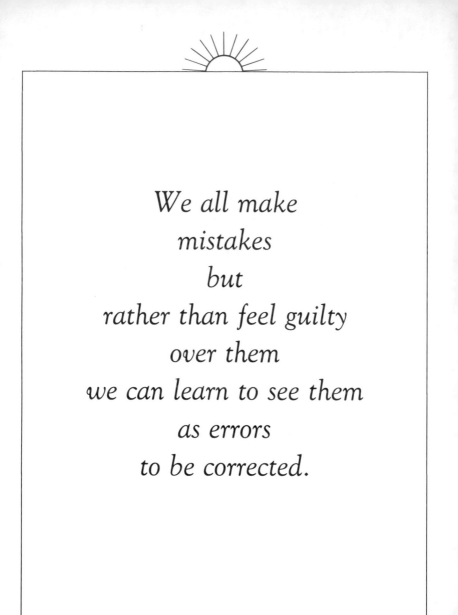

*We all make
mistakes
but
rather than feel guilty
over them
we can learn to see them
as errors
to be corrected.*

**Today I will attempt to
understand that there is no value
in holding onto grievances
and I will ask for help in
letting them go.**

Grievances and Love cannot co-exist together.
To be awakened is to see no value in holding onto grievances, and to ask our Higher Power for help in letting all of them go. To let go of all of our grievances, no matter how justified they may seem, is a decision to let go of suffering.

*For many of us
the people it's hardest
to forgive
are our parents.*

I am willing to forgive
my parents today.

Whether dead or alive, it is possible to forgive our parents totally for whatever harm we may think they did to us. To forgive doesn't mean to agree with or support their behavior. It simply means a willingness to live in the present by letting go of the past.

It may be helpful to remember that regardless of what we think our parents may have done to us, and no matter how repugnant their behavior might have been, it is just possible that if we had the same upbringing and life experiences that they did, we might have behaved similarly. It is possible to believe that our parents did the best job they knew how to do, based on their own, often miserable and hurtful, life experiences.

*When we think we are upset
with someone in the present,
it is often only a projection
from an unhealed conflict
in our past.*

I am never upset for the reason I think.*

When we find we are upset about someone or something that is happening in the present, it can be helpful to go inside and find where we may be holding on to similar feelings from an experience in the past. We can ask the question: "When did I first experience this same feeling?" We may then discover who or what we have originally not forgiven. Forgiveness for the past may be necessary before we can totally deal with the present.

Most of us are not totally aware of how much time we spend going through life playing the game of blame.

Today I choose to be a "Love finder" rather than a "fault finder."

Rather than looking at the negative side of life and being a fault finder, we can look at the positive side and be a Love finder. Rather than looking for darkness in others, we can look for the light and see that light as a reflection of our own. We can choose to let go and no longer see any value in playing the self-destructive game of blame.

*There will be no more cries
when everyone believes
that no one truly dies.*

Today I am willing to look at death differently.

Perhaps our biggest fear in life has been death because we have mistakenly believed that our only identity was limited to the body. Let us be willing to look at death differently remembering that "I am not a body. I am free. For I am still as God created me." *

Let us remind ourselves that as God's Creation of Love, we are everlasting, never ending, and eternal. Let us strive to remember that life and the body are not the same; and hence, there need be no fear when the body is put to rest.

*Love is the music that
gently awakens us
from the sleep
of forgetfulness
that what we are is
Love.*

When I get stuck in my head,
I will remember that
it is music that can set me free.

Music is the medicine God has given us to heal and nourish ourselves and to see the world differently. Music allows us to stop our analytical process and move to another dimension. Today let us remember that there is an ancient melody that abides in our hearts and let us choose to hear the music of Love.

What is important in life
is
the content of our hearts
and
not the form or score sheets
of our
achievements and performance.

Today I choose to burn up all my measuring sticks for others and myself.

Many of us have experienced Love by how well we have performed. This enforces the illusion that Love can be bought, bargained and traded. When we stop measuring Love, we allow it to flow naturally to and through all that is.

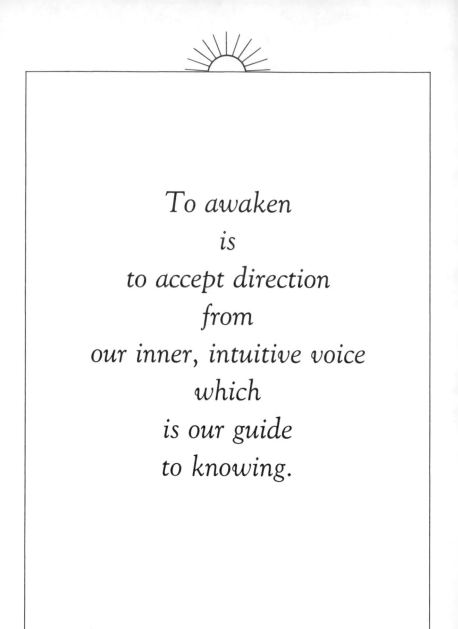

*To awaken
is
to accept direction
from
our inner, intuitive voice
which
is our guide
to knowing.*

Today I will learn to be still and ask the voice within what I should think, say and do.

We often make decisions based on the fearful, hurtful experiences of the past without consciously being aware of it. Today let us choose to have all our thoughts, words and actions come from Love as we learn to trust our Inner Voice of Love to guide us.

*We are most awake
when our minds
are still.*

**Today, for at least
10 minutes in the morning
and 10 minutes at night,
I will be willing to do my best
to empty my mind of all my
busy thoughts.**

There is an old Indian statement that a busy mind is a sick mind; a slow mind is a healthy mind; and, a still mind is a Divine Mind.

It is a still mind that is an awakened mind. It is a still mind that is an alert mind. It is a still mind that is a mind that is full of boundless Love. Let us see the value of having a quiet mind, and in stilling our minds in order that we may experience the fullness of Love.

Every time you forgive,
a new star
of Light
is
born.

Today I will light up the world through my forgiveness.

It is difficult for many of us to believe that the roots of darkness, conflicts, wars, poverty and unhappiness are our unforgiving thoughts. Each of us has a part to play in bringing more light to the world. Let us help each other remember through our own example that it only takes one second to forgive and bring light to an often darkened world.

When we are only loving
and kind,
this will be the sign that
we have learned to
still our minds.

Today being loving and kind will be my message for the day.

Empty your head of all that was said. Let go of all that you have read, and forget all that you have been fed or that there is any truth that you will ever be dead. Keep only the thought of Love, and Love is where you will be led.

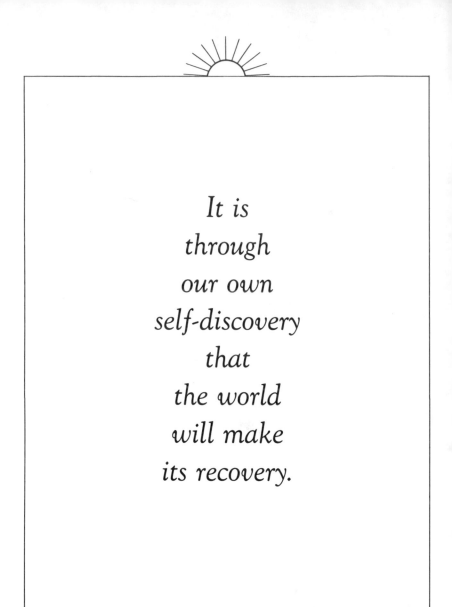

*It is
through
our own
self-discovery
that
the world
will make
its recovery.*

I will devote today to self-discovery.

Our egos would have us look outside of ourselves for the solutions to both the world's and our own personal problems. To wake up is to become aware that we have been looking in the wrong place and to go inside for all our directions and solutions.

Perhaps the world would be
in a better state
if
we spent more time focused
on
the contents of our hearts
rather
than on the shape and size
of our bodies.

Rather than focusing only on my body today, I am going to spend time purifying my heart and mind.

Our newspapers, magazines, television and radio programs consistently emphasize and focus on the body, tempting us to try to change our shape and size to be like someone else! If the amount of time that we spent on our body was focused on purifying the thoughts in our mind and our heart, the world and all of us in it would immediately feel better.

*Deep inside we all
long for Love;
and yet it is
perhaps
the fear of intimacy
that keeps
us from it.*

I will let go of my fear of intimacy, and be willing to let others "in-to-me-see." **

We become very afraid when we hold onto guilt, shame, anger and fear. We are afraid to be close to others because we feel unlovable and fearful that we will be attacked. We all make mistakes; and, it is important that we forgive ourselves and others and stop punishing each other.

Let us not be afraid to let others see and feel our inner core and to be truly vulnerable. Sharing our hearts with each other is the true essence of sharing Love.

*It is our loving hearts,
not our politicians,
that will transform
the world.*

**I will remember that
it is the love in my heart
that helps to transform
the world.**

We tend to give other people the responsibility of taking care of things and bringing positive changes about. We have received a
"wake up" call when we know that the responsibility lies in each of us, and that the vehicle for
such change is the transformation that takes place
within our own loving hearts.

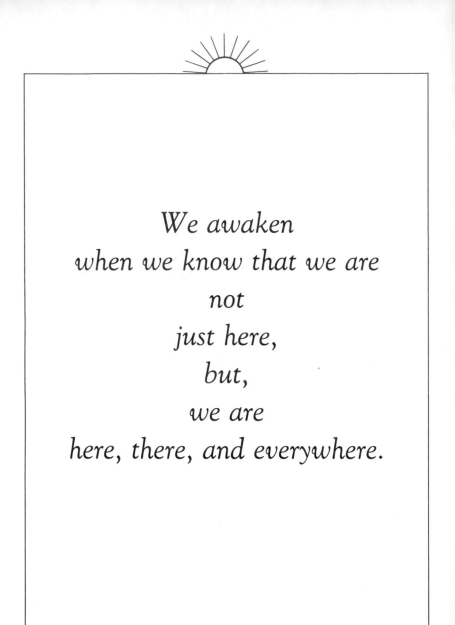

We awaken
when we know that we are
not
just here,
but,
we are
here, there, and everywhere.

I will be unrushed and truly present with everyone I meet today.

It is fear that keeps us hurried and in a rush. We make such big lists of all the things that we think we are supposed to accomplish that we frequently end the day breathless and worried. We seem to be so busy running that we miss out in experiencing the beauty of the present moment.

Today, let us see value in slowing down our pace, and let us approach each moment with an unhurried stillness. Let us concentrate on being totally attentive to whoever we meet and not be preoccupied with what we have been doing or what we have to do next. Let us remember that since our being is Love, our Love is here, there, and everywhere.

*Age is a question
of mind over matter.
If you don't mind
it doesn't matter.***

Today I will embrace my age and know that it is the perfect time for me.

Let us release ourselves from any anxiety about our age and celebrate that we are all in our perfect year. Releasing ourselves from our fears about aging allows us to experience pure joy each day.

As we celebrate the agelessness of our true spiritual self, our age can enhance, instead of limit, our zest, enthusiasm and passion for life.

Perhaps the whole world
would be released from pain
if each of us would take
the responsibility
of letting go of all
of our unforgiving thoughts.

When I am upset
I will remind myself that I am holding an unforgiving thought and I will choose to let it go.

It is our egos that generate all fear and unforgiving thoughts. They create the perception that God, the world, and everyone in it are unloving and unlovable and deserve our anger and our wrath. It is our unforgiving thoughts that cause us to see a fearful world that is filled with separateness and consumed by greed, attack, unfairness, and an absence of Love. Today we can do our part in choosing to see a world of oneness where there is only Love by seeing no value in our unforgiving thoughts.

*True trust
is faith
that will
never rust.*

**Today I will not be a
doubting Thomas
and I am willing to trust
the Love that created me
with an unwavering faith.**

Trust is an ancient memory of Love that is experienced deep within us. It has nothing to do with what our physical senses tell us or with our behavior. It has to do with a willingness to recognize the Light of Love in our Eternal Source, others, and ourselves.

*Perhaps our fear of Love
is what causes us to wreck
so many of our relationships.*

I will not be afraid of Love today.*

We have egos that treasure our past hurts and rejections. They tell us that relationships are not safe, we really can't trust others not to hurt 'and reject us, and that we should learn from our past experiences that we should be afraid of Love. Today is the day that I will not listen to my ego voice. Instead I will listen to the Inner Voice and trust in Love.

*Unconditional Love
is free of judgments and
condemnation.*

Today I will love unconditionally and see beyond the form and actions of others.

We are loving ourselves and others when we do not allow ourselves to be abused by participating in another's insane behavior. Unconditional love does not mean supporting another person's insanity. When we love unconditionally, we give up our judgments of others. We are then prepared to go inside and ask what it is we need to think, say and do about this relationship. The answer will then come from Love instead of anger, resentment, judgment and guilt.

*Love is always in
the air
when you take the time
to care.*

Today I will take the time to have a caring attitude towards others.

We live in a world where many of us have lost sight of our priorities of what is really important in life. We so often get caught in selfish interests and do an endless list of meaningless things. So many of us have spent dark nights of the soul because we have forgotten that the essence of life comes from caring for each other.

*When experiencing nature
becomes
as important as our breathing,
our souls
become nourished.*

I will nourish my soul by being in nature and being at one with it.

Is it possible that all the solutions to life's problems lie in nature? Is it possible that within nature lies all the secrets to the mysteries of life? And is it possible that by keeping our hands in the soil we make a soul connection with God?

Trees are wise spiritual teachers
that can teach us
the secrets of life.

I will find time to hug at least one tree today.

Have you ever noticed that trees are never in a hurry and know very well the secret of stillness and quiet? They are master teachers of patience and tranquility. They know how sturdy they can be when they hold their heads straight into the sky and they are smart enough to be flexible to any wind that may come by. They are very giving with their blossoms and shade, and are wise teachers of what life is all about. They give bundles of Love to all of life and are most deserving of our loving embrace.

To live a life and be awakened
is to live a life of Love.

To live a life of Love
is to live a life of surrender.

To live a life of surrender
is to live a life in which
Love is all
that you remember.

**I will be awakened today
and live a life of surrender,
in which Love is all
that I will remember.**

Let us this day join each other in Love. Let Love be our guiding light wherever we are. Let no one including ourselves be excluded from our Love. Let us surrender to Love so that it permeates our every breath and heartbeat, our every thought and action.

*Every moment is a new
opportunity to experience
life anew through
the Creator's Love.*

Today I will let go
of trying to get other people
to fit into my molds
for them.

We can stop basing our Love for others on how they act or how they perform. We can stop interpreting their behavior and being the judge of whether they are guilty or innocent. When we stop forcing others to fit into our molds, loving relationships become limitless.

The best way to navigate
through life
is to give up all
of our
controls.

**Today I will take that
leap in faith
and let the voice of
Love guide
my life.**

We try to control others when we feel insecure about ourselves. When we let go of trying to mold others into the shape that our egos wish them to take, we learn to trust and have faith in the Guiding Force in our lives that always directs us with Love.

*Nature isn't just an
environment
that we live within,
but an
aspect of
ourselves
expressed throughout.*

**When I remember that
I am part of all that there is,
I begin to take better care
of everything,
both inside and outside of myself.**

Nature remains as our teacher to continually awaken us to the beauty, harmony and transformation that evolves around us. It reminds us of the interconnectedness of all that inhabits this planet, thereby allowing us the opportunity to care for all that is living as if it were ourselves . . . for it is.

One of the biggest joys
we experience in this world
is when we lend
a helping hand to
another person.

The quality of my life will be determined by how much I give to others.

There is an old saying that states, "A volunteer is someone who reaches their hand out into the darkness to help another hand back into the Light, only to discover that it is their own."**

Let us focus on reaching out to give a helping hand wherever we may be. As we expand our hearts, we experience the greatest joy by embracing ourselves.

If we truly believe in equality, we need to live in such a way that it is demonstrated in every aspect of our lives.

**Today, by truly seeing everyone
as my equal,
regardless of their
age, sex, or experience,
I will be setting
them and myself free.**

We can see everyone as our teacher today. When we do not see ourselves as superior to others, we become student/teacher and teacher/student to each other, knowing that there is much that we can learn from everyone that we meet.

Being acutely aware of our thoughts allows us to guard against any old ways of thinking in which we may have demonstrated inequality by our words or actions.

The end of loneliness
comes
when you trust in the
continuous presence
of God
in your life.

When I am willing to feel the presence of God, I will not be lonely.

When we are willing to believe in another reality other than our physical one, there will be no such thing as loneliness and feelings of separation. When we believe in what we cannot see, feel or touch, we will recognize that we do not need bodies to communicate. When we recognize that minds can communicate by themselves, and that there is a universal mind that we are all a part of, then the illusion of loneliness disappears.

The biggest present
we
can give ourselves
is
to live in the present.

Today I will give myself the gift of living in the present.

Whether we choose to live in the past, present, or future is always a choice. What we choose depends on our belief system of what we believe will benefit us. We choose our belief system and what thoughts we put into our minds. When we not only believe, but know in the very depths of our being that we experience the presence of God only in the present, the decision to live in the present is made effortlessly.

One of the most beautiful
aspects of children
is their innocence
which can remind us
of our own.

Today I will rediscover the innocent child that still lives within me.

Many of us have blocked from our awareness the purity of the innocent child that rests within us. Instead, we have planted seeds that grow into the dark forest of guilt. We can choose to let go of our self-imposed guilt and let the innocence of the child within us shine.

When we look at adults, we tend to see only their costumes and masks. Putting it another way, we are attracted to their picture frame rather than the picture itself. We can always choose to see the innocent child in others, which can in turn serve to remind us of our own innocence.

*Spiritual uplifting occurs
the moment we love and respect
all of the animal kingdom
as if they were ourselves.*

Today is a day of my spiritual renewal because I will spend the day loving and respecting the animal kingdom.

It is so easy for us to take animals and insects for granted and not realize that they are living organisms too. Until we Love all of life equally, we will be spiritually empty. Perhaps we will not be able to feel whole until we are able to treat all that is living with Love, respect, and dignity.

There is a Light
that
shines in each of us
that
does away with
all darkness.

Let me look beyond the masks of everyone I meet and see only the Light of Love.

Our true selves reflect the Light of God's Love shining away all darkness and joining us as one. Our egos would have us see only the behavior of others which often can be a form of darkness and fear. What we see is based on our belief. We can choose what we believe. Therefore, we can choose to see only the light of Love that abides in us all.

*To be able to experience
peace and Love in its fullness,
forgiveness must become
as essential and continuous
as breathing.*

Today I will look upon everyone I see as a teacher of forgiveness.

Our egos would like us to see many people that we meet as potential enemies who do unforgiving things. It makes us believe that we are here to determine other people's guilt and to sentence them by keeping our Love from them.

Another way of looking at the world is to see everyone as our teacher of forgiveness. We cannot be at peace until all our relationships are healed. Not even one person can be excluded for us to experience complete inner peace. We need to remember that 90% of forgiveness doesn't work, it has to be 100%. It's like being pregnant. You are either pregnant or you are not.

Solitude is a friend,
not an enemy.
Learn to treasure, trust,
and enjoy it.

**Today I will be motivated
to have some periods of solitude
for myself
and I will make solitude
my dear friend.**

Let us not be afraid of solitude and being alone today or being afraid of our thoughts. We can welcome the opportunity to make friends with ourselves and the universe in the quietness of the moment.

*Many problems seem
impossible to solve because
we concentrate on the problem
rather than on the solution.*

**I will concentrate on the
solution of Love today,
and trust that by so doing,
what I thought were problems
will begin to be resolved.**

In the past it seems that we have lived in a world
where, at times, problems and conflicts oc-
curred that have seemed impossible to solve. Today is going to be different. Let us not believe in
the word "impossible," but be willing to believe
that Love is the answer to all the problems that
we may perceive that we have.

If each of us believed
that laughter was every bit
as important as eating,
we would all be walking around
much lighter, healthier,
and happier.

Today I am determined to have at least three meals of laughter about myself or some situation.

Let us not be so nearsighted that we miss the funny side of life. Let us concentrate on having a sense of humor today, and to have a willingness to laugh with passion with all of our bodies, just as babies teach us to do. We can learn to see the joy and freedom that comes from laughing with all of our being.

The greatest and most
significant changes for the
betterment of the world
occur when human beings
choose to have two openings:
open minds and
open hearts.

Today I will expand the openings in my mind and in my heart.

Let us be willing to take a new look at all values we hold dear to our hearts and have an open mind to all new thoughts, ideas and beliefs. Let us be willing to have our hearts open to giving and receiving Love by letting go of all judgments we have against other people and ourselves.

*Perhaps it is better to
go through life being
playful than as
a
workaholic.*

Today I am going to be playful and loving rather than hiding all my thoughts in my workaholism.

There are many of us who hide our thoughts from ourselves by spending all of our time working. It is almost as if we are afraid of our thoughts. It is important to have balance and not to be overly serious all the time. Let this be a playful and lighthearted day.

*A truly creative person
rids him or herself of all
self-imposed
limitations.*

This is the day I will open my heart and mind to the fire of creative energy by letting go of all my self-imposed limitations.

Today we can let go of all our old beliefs of what we think we can or cannot do. Using an imaginary paint brush we can paint a picture of what our hearts would have us do to bring the most joy and Love to the world and to ourselves, and do it. This is the day for empowering ourselves to not believe in the impossible, but to believe in our dreams.

When we are depressed,
somewhere deep inside
we ultimately
are
denying
the
Presence of God.

**If for any reason
I should feel depressed today,
I will remind myself that
I can choose to remember God.**

Each day we can remind ourselves of the joy we experience when we remember that we are always joined with the heart of God. When we are upset or depressed, the bottom line is that we have separated ourselves, have failed to remember, and have lost faith and trust in God's Love.

*You will never run
out of gas when you use
"soular" energy.*

Today I will feel
God's boundless, loving energy
running through my veins.

When we are inspired by God we are energized by an unstoppable energy. It is our soul connection with God that vitalizes, invigorates and allows us to soar beyond our imagination.

Just as silence
is
the footprint of God,
chatter, noise
and the
busyness of the world
are
the footprints of the ego.

Today I am willing to find the peace of God through silence.

Treasuring silence reminds us that the highest state of Love needs no words. In that silence, we can find the presence of the peace of God.

If every step that everyone took was a step toward forgiveness, there would only be peace.

My function today is to make every step I take one of forgiveness.

We live in a society that often thinks it is sane and healthy to be unforgiving. Let us change that today by remembering that the only way to sanity and health is through forgiveness and Love.

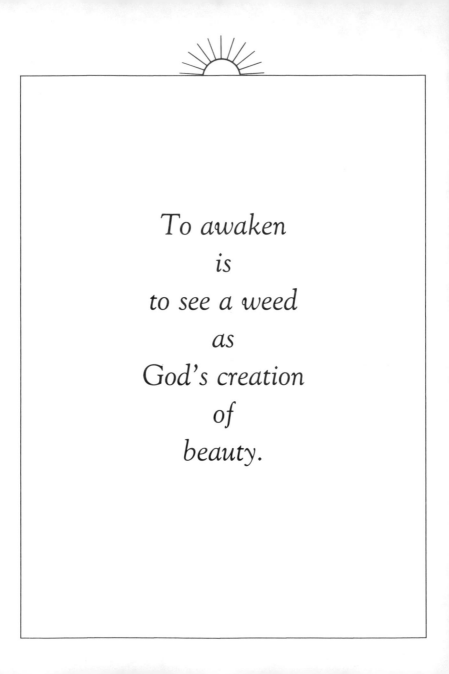

To awaken
is
to see a weed
as
God's creation
of
beauty.

I choose to not limit my Love by appreciating all that has been created.

We live in a world that seems to believe that a rose is more beautiful than a weed. It is only the ego that categorizes and makes comparisons. The world of God's Love has to do with content of Love, not form. Let us Love our own, as well as others' so-called "imperfections." Let us see only the content of Love reflecting light in all that is, regardless of the form.

In order to get where you
want to go,
you
first have to leave where
you are at.**

I am willing to be open to change today.

It is so easy to become rigidly stuck in our belief systems and to become resistant to any change. To live in this world successfully we need to become flexible like the limbs of a tree and learn to bend in the wind, all the while keeping a firm footing in the ground.

*We can always learn from
any situation we are
currently involved in,
no matter how undesirable
it may appear.*

**It is my desire to remember
that I can look on everything
that happens to me today
as a positive lesson
God would have me learn.**

No matter what happens today, we can choose to not see ourselves as a victim acting as if God is throwing bricks at us from heaven. We can choose to have faith and trust that everything that happens to us is, ultimately a positive lesson God would have us learn.

Children
who see and speak to fairies,
or have imaginary playmates,
are not crazy.
They
simply are showing us
the way.

Today I will explore the world through my imagination.

We have limited our reality by thinking things have to be seen by our physical eyes, and touched, weighed and measured in order to be real. We have, unfortunately, forgotten the children's world that we were once in, where we could believe in what was invisible, and where the reality of our imaginary world became just as real, if not more so than the physical world. Let us learn from children about a new reality that creative imagination can bring to us. Once again we can remember that "A little child shall lead us."

Forgiveness is giving up
all hopes
*for a better past.***

The secret of positive, loving relationships in the present is to heal the unhealed relationships in our past.

There are many strong teachers of forgiveness that come into our lives, offering us new opportunities to make a choice between judging and condemning or forgiving and loving. Each moment of our lives is for choosing once again.

We often keep alive our pain from the past and relive it as if it is still happening today. In reality, the incident will never change; only our perception of it will.

*Perhaps we do have
invisible
wings because when
we are
full of love, it feels
like we can
fly.*

I'm going to flap my wings today by keeping my heart fueled with Love.

When we feed ourselves with anger and guilt, we weigh ourselves down.

Have you ever noticed how gravity seems to disappear and how much lighter we feel when we are concentrating on helping others by giving our Love away?

A garbage disposal for our minds would do much to help clean up the environment and to cleanse and uplift the face of the world.

**Today I will remember
that it is my own thoughts
that determine the world I see
and by doing so,
I take responsibility for myself
and for the planet.**

Thoughts of negativity, anger, hate, jealousy, possessiveness, fear and guilt keep us from experiencing who and what we are. They make us fearful of Love and cause us to trash out our relationships. Those who trash out their relationships tend to trash out the environment too. Let us imagine that we have a garbage disposal in our minds and every time we are tempted to have a negative thought, we can press the button and dispose of it.

Gratitude is not a platitude.
It is
a
way of life.

I awaken this day with gratitude for all I have been given.

A day lived in gratitude for everything that happens to us, even though we might not understand it and it might not have been in our plan, is a day where inner peace is experienced. As we learn something positive from every experience we have, we are later able to help others because of that experience.

*The secret of
experiencing joy
is to feel
worthy of happiness.*

I will experience
the joy of happiness today
because happiness is
my inheritance
and my natural state.

We have been brought up in a world that equated and made Love conditional on how well we performed. Who has as both a child and an adult not been bombarded with thousands upon thousands of "I will Love you if's." Many of us have become fearful of Love because we are afraid that we will be rejected. We often evaluate others with our many measuring sticks instead of nourishing them with Love.

Today, we can choose to refrain from the temptation of using measuring sticks with other people as well as with ourselves. It is our inheritance from God.

Age is an attitude.
It can be a number
that severely restricts and
limits us,
or it can be
meaningless and
not limit us
in any way.

**I will remind myself
that I can always be
young in heart
by keeping a child's
wonderment, curiosity and awe
within my heart.**

Let us remind ourselves that the contents of our hearts and minds can always be young and ageless in spirit. We can always be helpful and useful to others, no matter what the state of our bodies are. And if we feel we have to count, let us count only our smile wrinkles, and not our age wrinkles.

Would you consider that
it might be better
to be irrational
and love than
to be rational and hate?

**Today I am going to forget
about labels such as
rational and irrational
and I am going to choose to love.**

We live in a society that loves to categorize
people. We do not have to let ourselves be
categorized and we can refuse to categorize ourselves. Love is not a category. It is all that there is.

When we put our heartprints
on each other
rather than our footprints,
we will have created a
different world.

**Today I will devote time
to opening my heart
with Love and compassion,
and to leave the gentle
imprints of my heart on others
through offering them a hug.**

We live in a world that often seems to be filled with competition and greed. People seem to frequently be climbing over each other, stepping on each other, trying to get to the top, only to find that what they were looking for was not to be found there.

Let us remind each other that God invented hugging to bring two hearts together as one. Hugging allows for soul connections to take place. It is only when our hearts are closed off to Love by fear that we begin to step on each other—leaving the scars of our footprints. It is absolutely amazing and spectacular how quickly hugging can dissolve away old scars.

To be silly, to giggle,
and to be joy-filled
is a cardinal sign
of maturity revealing
that you have let the child
in you
come out and play.

Today I will be willing
to do something that is
silly and outrageous
and will give up all my old ideas
about what maturity
may or may not be.

We live in a strange world that seems attached to strange beliefs. We believe that the older we get, the more serious we should become; the older we get, the more weight we should have on our shoulders. We believe the aging process should bring more worries. We believe that it is only the young who can have the luxury of being light-hearted; and that with maturity comes the weight of a heavy heart. We even tend to believe that maturity means more accuracy in deciding who is guilty and who is innocent.

Today is the day to open the door to our heart and let our child come out and play.

Each of us has significant,
crucial and equal roles
to play
in the healing of the world.

**I am determined
to live a meaningful life
by contributing something
each and every day
to the betterment of the world.**

Let us recognize the importance of asking our-selves each day what we can do to bring more Love and peace into the world. Let us try not to compare what we do with others and remember that each gift of Love has equal importance regardless of how small or large that gift may seem to be.

The secret of inner and
outer success
is to love
all others as ourselves.

I will love all others today as myself.

There are many of us that have experienced outside success, but have still felt empty inside. Outer success often is obtained through the ego's motivation of "getting" and we may remain empty inside because we have not been truly focused on "giving" to others with all of our heart. It is almost as if we were concerned primarily about ourselves and that the people around us became objects.

Today, let us remember that the secret of inner success is caring, helping, and loving others with the same energy and focus that we have for ourselves and our family.

*Darkness occurs
when we witness each other's
fear,
while Light begins to emerge
when we witness each other's
Love.*

Today I choose to be a witness to the Light in others.

We choose what thoughts we put into our mind. We choose what we see and what we experience. Let us be willing to unlearn our old "robot" ways of immediately reacting with fear to other people's fears. Today let us choose to use spiritual vision and be witnesses of the Light of Love in each other.

The wisdom of nature
can give us all the answers
to our day-to-day problems
and show us the way
to heal ourselves.

**I will blend with
the silent vibrations of nature
by seeing value in escaping
from my hurried and busy world.**

Making our love for nature as important as breathing and eating can lead us to experience the place of stillness within us.

We will know and experience
a fuller meaning of the
word Love
when everyone we meet
becomes our
teacher of patience.

I will remind myself that patience and Love are one and the same.

Is your patience limited? Do you find it difficult to wait? Does your impatience lead to a feeling of justified anger? If we agree that patience and Love are one and the same, then perhaps we would be willing to let every person we meet, or every situation we encounter or even think about, be our teacher of patience.

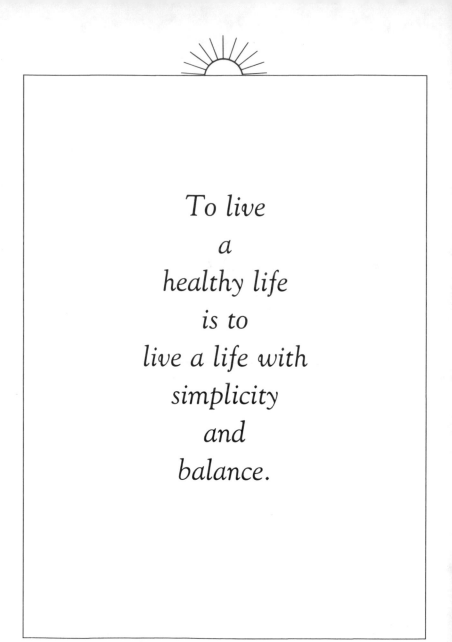

*To live
a
healthy life
is to
live a life with
simplicity
and
balance.*

**Today I will look at my lifestyle
and strive to change things
in order that I may
live a more harmonious life.**

Much of the stress we have is due to the fact that we have created very complex lifestyles for ourselves. Many of our illnesses are caused by stress. If we look at our bodies, many of us are walking around in a tilt position. Many of us live in a cement environment and have lost our connections with the rhythms of the earth. Today is the day to simplify and take the complexitics out of our lives.

The world is
right side up
when being
is as important
as achieving.

**Today I will still my mind
and recognize that achieving
has nothing to do with how
loved I am,
or how much love
I am capable of giving.**

In our natural state of being, our love continues to extend and expand. Our thoughts are just as important as our actions. Let this be a day of learning how to just be. Let us remember that God loves us for the essence of our being and not for what we may or may not have achieved.

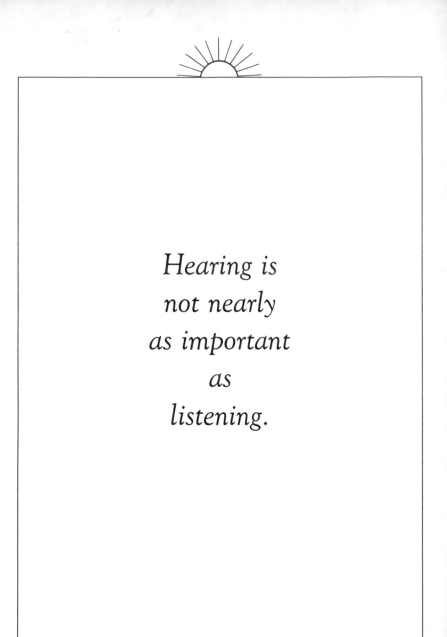

*Hearing is
not nearly
as important
as
listening.*

Today I am willing to be a good listener.

There is a person who was a volunteer that we met in New Zealand. She had one word under her name which said everything about her—"Listener." She was there to give her unconditional love by listening. She was not there to give advice, opinions, make judgments, or change others.

Let us wear, today, an invisible sign that says, "Listener."

There is a child
in everyone of us
that needs to be continuously
nurtured.

Today I will take time to nourish and love the fearful child in me.

Although we are born as innocent, happy children, it doesn't take too long for most of us to experience what it's like to be fearful. Many of us keep this fearful child image alive within our minds as adults. That fearful child may have been rejected and abused and can pop out at any time. We are the best ones available to heal the fearful child that may be within us through our awareness and our Love and forgiveness. Let us use our imagination today and hold the fearful child within us closely with comfort, Love and compassion.

*Relationships fail
when
we try to write
scripts
for them.*

I will experience peace every time I tear up the script I have written for another person.

Our egos continue to tell us that our job in relationships is to change the other person so that she or he will behave in a way that meets our approval. So we go through life trying to change others and end up frustrated and in conflict because of our lack of success. When we awaken, we recognize that we are here in this world to Love one another, not change each other. Today, let us carefully watch ourselves to see if we are writing scripts for others. If we are, we can tear them up because we want to experience peace.

The world would be more peaceful if we spent our energy taking down fences rather than putting them up.

Today I am willing to dissolve all barriers between myself and others.

We build up so many barriers between ourselves, others, and our Source. Every thought of blame, revenge, and justified anger creates a wall between ourselves and others, and between ourselves and Love. Barriers are the ego's blocks to Love. Bill Thetford once said that "A miracle is a shift in perception that removes the blocks to the awareness of Love's presence." The miracle of Love is experienced when we remove our self-imposed blocks.

*We often overfeed
our bodies
while
undernourishing
our souls.*

Today I will be conscious of what I feed myself.

The quantity and quality of food that we place in our bodies is often a reflection of other attitudes we hold about ourselves. We sometimes get our hungers mixed up by confusing spiritual hunger with the hunger for food. We overeat because we feel empty of Love and because Love has escaped us. When we feed our souls with Love and gratitude, we have no need to overeat.

Are you willing
to
think of someone
you
have not forgiven
and
forgive them
today?

I am willing to forgive at least one person today that I am holding a grievance against.

Our egos are so stubborn and tell us, "What that person did was unforgivable. Never forgive them or you will be hurt again."

Our egos will do anything to keep us in conflict and pain to keep us away from peace and joy. We always have a choice of whether to listen to the voice of Love which tells us to Love and forgive, or the voice of the ego which tells us to condemn and not forgive. Let us truly commit ourselves to forgive at least one person today.

Is it possible that
when we are not at ease
that we may have dis-ease?

**Today I am willing to
remember that it may be
my unforgiving thoughts
that are at the roots of my
not feeling at ease,
and I will then see value
in forgiveness.**

When we choose not to carry "attack" thoughts in our mind, we become calm, tranquil, and we stop punishing our body. We can be at ease no matter what is happening. There is always a peaceful place inside of our hearts where we can rest and be calm. Let us not attack our bodies today with anger. Let us not only forgive others, but ourselves as well.

*To awaken is to know that
springtime and the sun
are always within us.*

Today I will be like the sun and wherever I go I will bring Springtime and the sun with me.

There is an indomitable spirit within each of us that is forever ready to blossom. With everyone we meet we can be a breath of fresh air. We can blossom with beauty and joy, and bring the energy of new birth to those who feel they are half frozen and half dead from the cold winter of isolation and rejection. Let us remember that Springtime is an attitude that reflects the warmth of the sun and the birth of a season of growth. Let every season be Springtime, the season of Love.

We feel weak
when
we think we have given
our power
away
to others.

Today I will respect the power within me.

We live in a world where it is very easy to give our power away to physicians, lawyers, politicians, our spouses, our children, our parents, and a host of other people. The greatest power in the world is Love and the power of Love always abides in us. When we feel fearful, we tend to give the control of our lives over to others to make decisions for us. The power of making decisions always is within us.

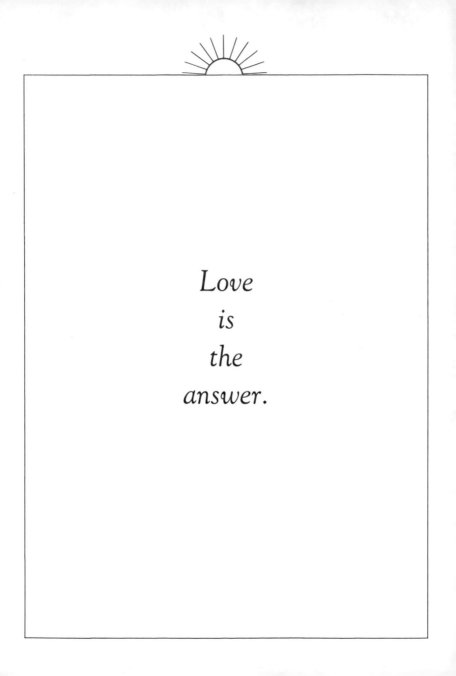

*Love
is
the
answer.*

Let me remember that Love is the answer to all my problems.

No matter what the question, Love is the answer. No matter what the pain or illness, Love is the answer. No matter what the loss, Love is the answer. No matter what the fear, Love is the answer.

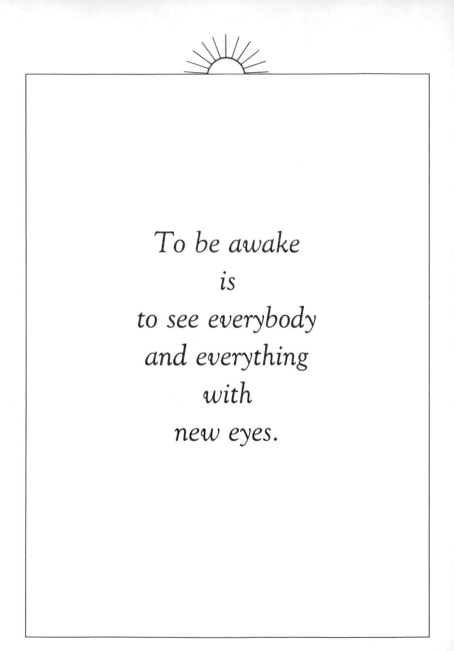

To be awake
is
to see everybody
and everything
with
new eyes.

Today I will look at all that I see, as if I had never seen it before.

Let us help each other be fully alive by looking at nature and each other with the feeling of discovery and freshness that comes with any experience as if it is our very first time. Let us resist comparisons and see the freshness of creative beauty in all that we behold.

If you are feeling ecstasy and your heart is pumping so fast it feels as if it is in your throat, if you are filled with awe and have goose bumps all over your body, and if your eyes are opened wide in wonderment, if you experience all these things from simply looking at a weed, you are beginning to awaken.

When you have a
passion
for compassion,
your Love will never be
rationed.

My own burning passion today is to be compassionate to all of life.

When we are awake we are aware that there is a fire of passion for compassion in our hearts that can never burn out. When we take down all of the picket fences around our hearts, we will find that being compassionate and kind is our natural state of being.

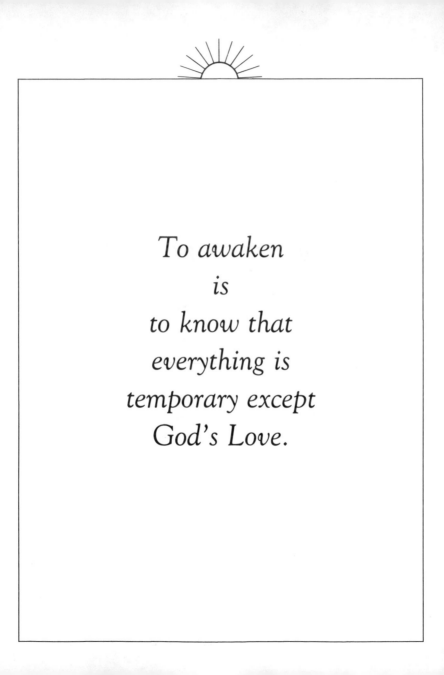

*To awaken
is
to know that
everything is
temporary except
God's Love.*

I will remember today that God's Love is all that is eternal.

The world that is limited by what we see with the physical eyes is a world of form that continues to change.

It is part of our illusion. A rule of thumb to go by is to remember that anything that changes belongs to the world of ego where everything changes, and that which doesn't change belongs to the world of Love. True Love is eternal, not temporary. Are we willing yet to consider that in the true world of Love, there is no past, no future, only the eternal now? The content of the real world is Love without form that is continuous and never ending.

We can tiptoe through life
with joy
when
we know that the world we
see
with our physical eyes
is
but a dream.

Today I am willing to wake up and see the world I have been seeing with my physical eyes as but a dream.

Our dear friend, author Hugh Prather once said that perhaps the holiest song ever written was, *"Row, Row, Row your boat, gently down the stream. Merrily, merrily, merrily, merrily, life is but a dream."*

We agree with Hugh. Today, let us join together and make our "wake-up" call, *"Row, Row, Row your boat, gently down the stream. Merrily, merrily, merrily, merrily, life is but a dream."*

*To the ego, life is a game of
hide and seek.
We hide the Love that is
always within us from ourselves,
and then we seek to find it
outside of ourselves
where it can never be found.*

Today I choose to have a willingness to believe that every aspect of my being is filled and overflowing with the abundance of Love.

No longer do we have to believe in the scarcity of Love within ourselves or feel an emptiness of spirit inside us. As Love, and as part of that which created us, we can remember that we have everything within ourselves to make us happy.

The "whys" of the past
are not as important
as the "whats"
of the present.

**Today I will let go
of all my "why" questions,
and I will ask endlessly the
"what" question:
"What can I do to be more
helpful and loving to others?"**

The "why" questions tend to keep us stuck in the intellectual analyses of the past which makes it very difficult for us to experience Love. The essence of life is in this present moment—and perhaps the most helpful challenging question we can ask ourselves is, "What can I do to bring about more joining and help and Love to others today?"

*Perhaps
puppy dogs
never have back pains
because
they are always
wagging their tails.*

Today,
rather than chasing my tail,
I am going to wag it
in happiness instead.

We all have a lot to learn from puppies. They know that they are here to be happy. They wag their tails all the time in happiness and their wagging increases in frequency the moment you hold them. Rather than chasing our tails through life, let us join each other and wag our tails. If we all wagged our tails, maybe we would have no more backaches.

*We are reminded of
our wholeness
when Love and forgiveness
become a never-ending process.*

I will experience wholeness today through my Love and forgiveness.

Our egos will tell us, "You can't Love everyone and some people do things that are unforgivable." Our egos will also tell us that we should not forgive.

The way to peace is not to listen to the ego, but to the voice of Love. It tells us that to find the peace of God, no one can be excluded from our Love and forgiveness. Since most of us have stubborn egos, Love and forgiveness needs to be a continuous process.

*When
we stop judging,
there will no
longer be any need for
forgiveness.*

Today I will contribute to the world through my forgiveness of myself and others.

When we forgive the world, what we see with our physical eyes may be totally transformed into a light whose brightness and beauty is beyond our imagination. We need to see the value in forgiving our religious training or the lack of such training; in forgiving our outdated concepts of God, the world, and all that is in it. We can then feel whole, joined, and at one once again.

*Your soul
longs
to greet
your
awakening.*

Today I will be open to the Spirit within me.

L et us feel today the joy that comes from opening up all of ourselves to the Spirit within. Let us celebrate life together as we ride on the wings of Love to heights that have no limits on the journey safely home.

EPILOGUE

May the inner alarm clock
that is in each of us continue
to ring loud and clear every day,
hour, minute and second
to awaken us to the magnitude,
beauty and power of Love
that is within each of us.

Personal Notes

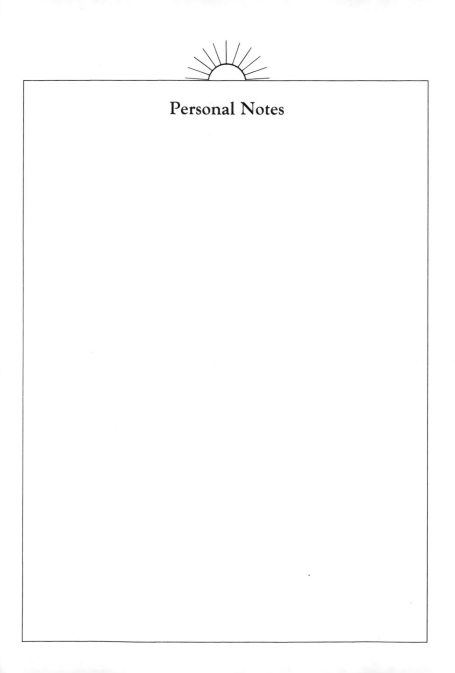

Personal Notes

Personal Notes

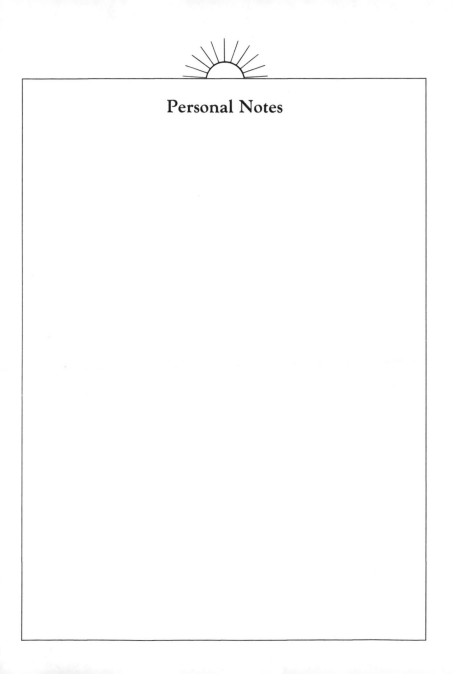

Personal Notes

Personal Notes

Personal Notes

Personal Notes

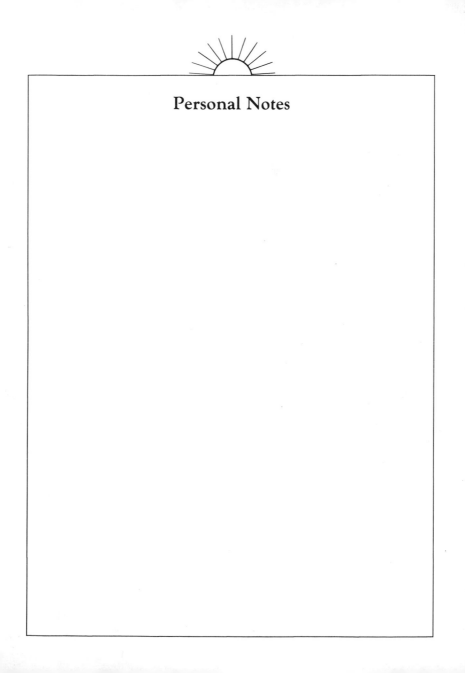

Personal Notes

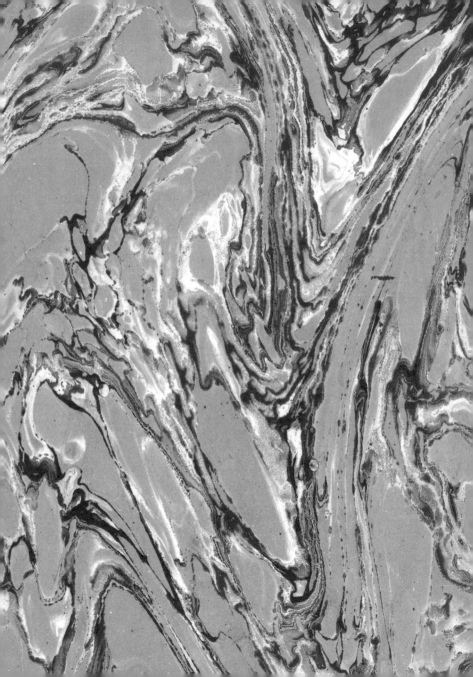